D1710174

Crystals

by Grace Hansen

GEOLOGY ROCKS!

Abdo Kids Jumbo is an Imprint of Abdo Kids
abdobooks.com

abdobooks.com

Published by Abdo Kids, a division of ABDO, P.O. Box 398166, Minneapolis, Minnesota 55439.
Copyright © 2020 by Abdo Consulting Group, Inc. International copyrights reserved in all countries.
No part of this book may be reproduced in any form without written permission from the publisher.
Abdo Kids Jumbo™ is a trademark and logo of Abdo Kids.

Printed in the United States of America, North Mankato, Minnesota.

052019

092019

Photo Credits: Alamy, iStock, Shutterstock

Production Contributors: Teddy Borth, Jennie Forsberg, Grace Hansen
Design Contributors: Dorothy Toth, Pakou Moua

Library of Congress Control Number: 2018963579

Publisher's Cataloging-in-Publication Data

Names: Hansen, Grace, author.

Title: Crystals / by Grace Hansen.

Description: Minneapolis, Minnesota : Abdo Kids, 2020 | Series: Geology rocks!
    set 2 | Includes online resources and index.

Identifiers: ISBN 9781532185564 (lib. bdg.) | ISBN 9781532186547 (ebook) |
    ISBN 9781532187032 (Read-to-me ebook)

Subjects: LCSH: Crystals--Juvenile literature. | Minerology--Juvenile
    literature. | Geology--Juvenile literature.

Classification: DDC 549--dc23

Table of Contents

Crystals

Crystals are hard **minerals**. They can be many shapes, sizes, and colors. To understand crystals, it is important to know about atoms.

4

Atoms are the building blocks of the universe. Earth, air, water, and everything around you are made of atoms!

There are around 90 different types of atoms that make up everything. They are called **elements**. Some **minerals** are also elements. Other minerals are made up of a few different atoms bonded together.

9

Gold, silver, and copper are examples of **elements**.

The atoms inside of a crystal form a **pattern**. The pattern repeats over and over again. The pattern of atoms gives crystals their shape.

13

Crystal Systems

There are six main shapes or crystal systems. The simplest and most common is the cube. Cubes have six **faces**. Yellow fluorite is a **mineral** that forms into a cube shape.

cube

Where & How They Form

Many crystals form in water. Others form from vapor or in molten rock. Amethyst forms under heat and **pressure**.

17

A crystal's color comes from the **minerals** it contains. Rubies are made from **corundum**. The red color comes from a bit of **chromium** mixed in.

Gemstones are rare crystals.

They are beautiful and strong.

They are made deep in the

earth. Diamonds and emeralds

are two kinds of gems.

Crystals & Crystal Systems

amethyst
hexagonal system

kyanite
triclinic system

salt
cubic system

sulfur
monoclinic system

topaz
orthorhombic system

zircon
tetragonal system

22

Glossary

chromium – a chemical element that is a hard and brittle metal.

corundum – a rock-forming mineral.

element – a pure substance made up of one kind of atom. Ninety elements occur naturally on Earth.

face – a front part or surface.

mineral – a substance, like gold, silver, or iron, formed in the earth that is not of an animal or plant.

pattern – an arrangement of shapes that is repeated again and again.

pressure – a steady force upon something.

23

Index

Abdo Kids
ONLINE
FREE! ONLINE MULTIMEDIA RESOURCES

Visit abdokids.com
to access crafts, games,
videos, and more!

Use Abdo Kids code

GCK5564

or scan this QR code!